AMAZING ORIGAMI

Flying Origami

Joe Fullman

Gareth Stevens
PUBLISHING

Please visit our website, www.garethstevens.com. For a free color catalog of all our high-quality books, call toll free 1-800-542-2595 or fax 1-877-542-2596.

Cataloging-in-Publication Data

Fullman, Joe.
Flying origami / by Joe Fullman.
p. cm. — (Amazing origami)
Includes index.
ISBN 978-1-4824-4155-0 (pbk.)
ISBN 978-1-4824-4156-7 (6-pack)
ISBN 978-1-4824-4157-4 (library binding)
1. Paper airplanes — Juvenile literature.
2. Origami — Juvenile literature. I. Fullman, Joe. II. Title.
TT870.F85 2016
736'.982—d23

First Edition

Published in 2016 by
Gareth Stevens Publishing
111 East 14th Street, Suite 349
New York, NY 10003

Copyright © 2016 Arcturus Publishing

Models and photography: Belinda Webster and Michael Wiles
Text: Joe Fullman
Design: Emma Randall
Editor: Frances Evans

Printed in the United States of America

CPSIA compliance information: Batch CW16GS: For further information contact Gareth Stevens, New York, New York at 1-800-542-2595.

Contents

Basic Folds

Origami has been popular in Japan for hundreds of years and is now loved all around the world. You can make great models with just one sheet of paper... and this book shows you how!

The paper used in origami is thin but strong, so that it can be folded many times. It is usually colored on one side. Alternatively you can use ordinary scrap paper, but make sure it's not too thick.

Origami models often share the same folds and basic designs. This introduction explains some of the folds that you will need for the projects in this book, and they will also come in useful if you make other origami models. When making the models in this book, follow the key below to find out what the lines and arrows mean. And always crease well!

KEY

valley fold ------------

mountain fold ···················

step fold (mountain and valley fold next to each other)

direction to move paper

push ◄

MOUNTAIN FOLD

To make a mountain fold, fold the paper so that the crease is pointing up towards you, like a mountain.

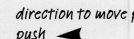
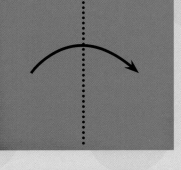

VALLEY FOLD

To make a valley fold, fold the paper the other way, so that the crease is pointing away from you, like a valley.

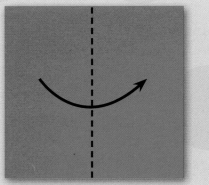

A NOTE ABOUT MEASUREMENTS

Measurements are given in U.S. form with the metric in parentheses. The metric conversion is rounded to make it easier to measure.

INSIDE REVERSE FOLD

An inside reverse fold is useful if you want to make a nose or a tail, or if you want to flatten off the shape of another part of an origami model.

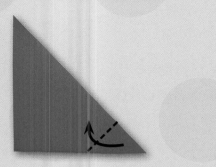

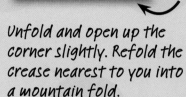

Open

1 Practice by first folding a piece of paper diagonally in half. Make a valley fold on one point and crease.

2 It's important to make sure that the paper is creased well. Run your finger over the crease two or three times.

3 Unfold and open up the corner slightly. Refold the crease nearest to you into a mountain fold.

4 Open up the paper a little more and then tuck the tip of the point inside. Close the paper. This is the view from the underside of the paper.

5 Flatten the paper. You now have an inside reverse fold.

OUTSIDE REVERSE FOLD

An outside reverse fold is useful if you want to make a head, beak or foot, or another part of your model that sticks out.

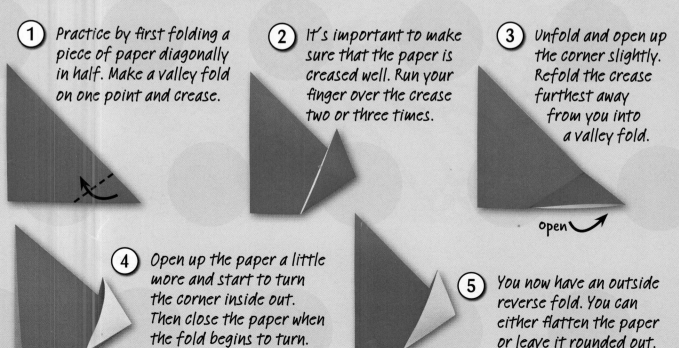

1 Practice by first folding a piece of paper diagonally in half. Make a valley fold on one point and crease.

2 It's important to make sure that the paper is creased well. Run your finger over the crease two or three times.

3 Unfold and open up the corner slightly. Refold the crease furthest away from you into a valley fold.

Open

4 Open up the paper a little more and start to turn the corner inside out. Then close the paper when the fold begins to turn.

5 You now have an outside reverse fold. You can either flatten the paper or leave it rounded out.

Fluttering Butterfly

Follow the steps to fold this beautiful butterfly and make it flutter from flower to flower. You could use felt-tip pens to draw patterns on the wings, so it looks just like a real butterfly.

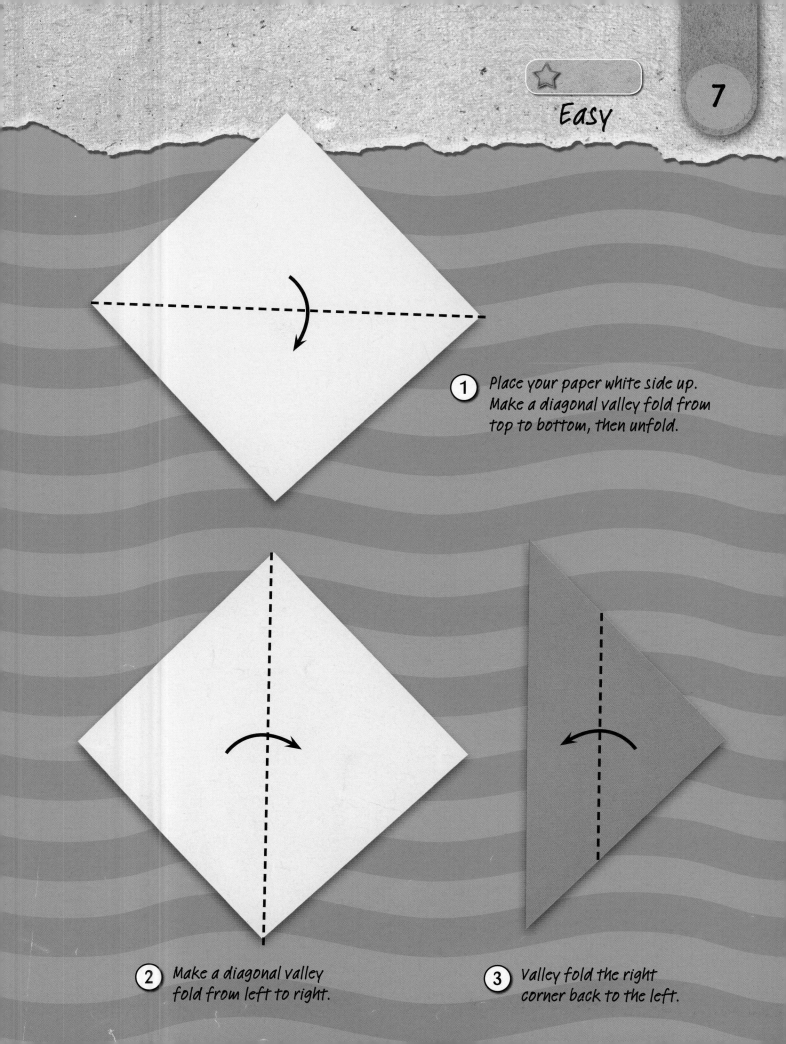

1 Place your paper white side up. Make a diagonal valley fold from top to bottom, then unfold.

2 Make a diagonal valley fold from left to right.

3 Valley fold the right corner back to the left.

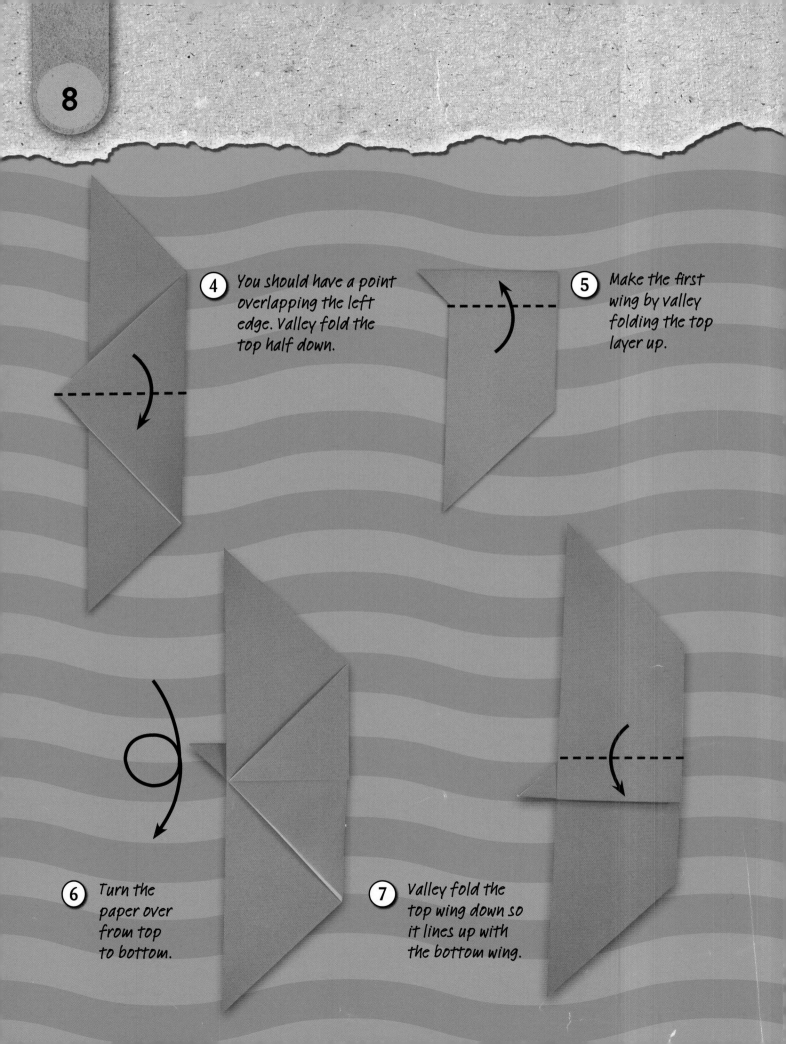

4 You should have a point overlapping the left edge. Valley fold the top half down.

5 Make the first wing by valley folding the top layer up.

6 Turn the paper over from top to bottom.

7 Valley fold the top wing down so it lines up with the bottom wing.

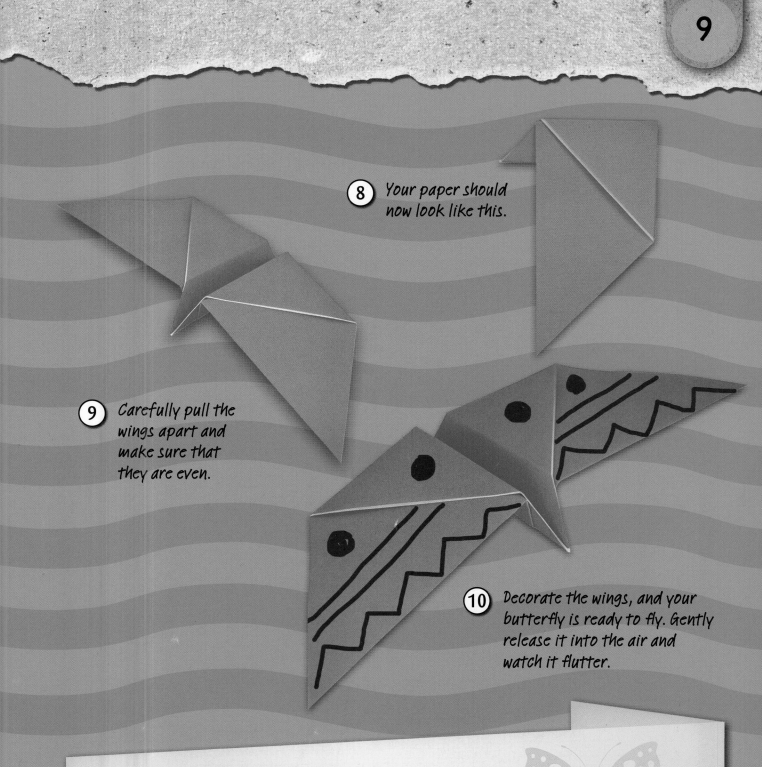

8 Your paper should now look like this.

9 Carefully pull the wings apart and make sure that they are even.

10 Decorate the wings, and your butterfly is ready to fly. Gently release it into the air and watch it flutter.

Did You Know?

Every year millions of monarch butterflies fly more than 3,000 miles (4,800 km) from the cold weather of the United States to the warmer temperature of Mexico.

10 Flying Kite

Easy

Up, up and away! This crazy kite really does fly. Just be sure to attach some string so that it doesn't blow away.

1. Valley fold the paper in half from left to right, forming a triangle.

2. Take the right-hand corner of the top layer of paper and fold it back to the center crease.

3. Your paper should look like this, with just a small colored triangle at the top.

4. Turn the paper over from left to right, then fold the left-hand corner over to the right edge.

⑤ Turn over and repeat on the other side. Then turn the paper back over.

⑥ Turn the paper over from right to left.

⑦ Fold the top edge of the white paper over so it lines up with the right-hand edge.

Did You Know?

Kites were invented by the Chinese more than 2,000 years ago. The earliest kites were made of silk and were used for sending messages.

8 Your paper should look like this.

 9 Carefully pull the folds out so the paper can stand upright.

 10 Use a hole punch to attach some string to your kite, head out on a windy day and see how high your kite can soar.

Flapping Bird

Different birds use their wings in different ways. While an eagle soars through the sky, a hummingbird flutters its tiny wings constantly. Here's how to make your own flapping bird!

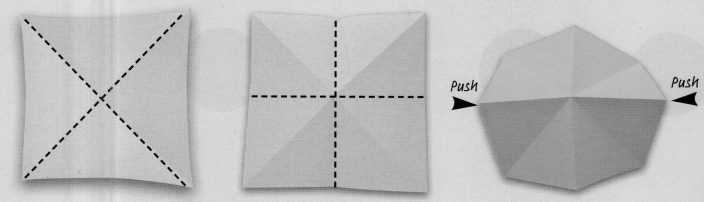

1 Place your paper as shown. Valley fold diagonally both ways.

2 Valley fold along the horizontal and vertical lines. Then turn your paper over.

3 Push the left- and right-hand corners together, so the shape starts to collapse.

Push   *Push*

4 Your model should now look like this. Flatten the top to create a square.

5 Valley fold the top right-hand layer to meet the center crease.

6 Do the same on the left-hand side.

7 Your model should look like this. Turn over and repeat steps 5 and 6 on the other side.

8 Valley fold the top flap down.

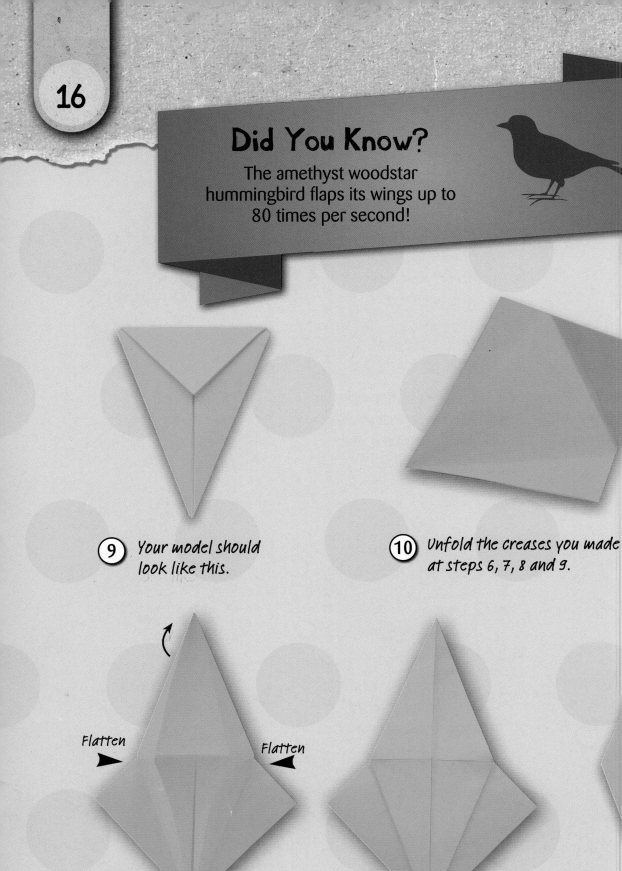

Did You Know?

The amethyst woodstar hummingbird flaps its wings up to 80 times per second!

9 Your model should look like this.

10 Unfold the creases you made at steps 6, 7, 8 and 9.

Flatten

Flatten

11 Gently lift the bottom flap upwards to make a pocket. Flatten the edges.

12 Your model should now look like this.

13 Turn your model over and repeat steps 11 and 12 on the other side.

14 Valley fold the right-hand point up.

15 Now, turn this last fold into an inside reverse fold. This is your bird's tail.

16 Valley fold the left-hand point up. Turn this into an inside reverse fold.

17 Valley fold the left-hand tip as shown, then make an inside reverse fold. This is your bird's head.

18 Valley fold the wing. Turn over and repeat to form the second wing.

19 To make the wings move, hold your bird's neck and pull on its tail. Your origami bird is ready to leave the nest!

Airplane

This sleek, streamlined plane is built for speed. Follow the instructions carefully to make sure it flies as fast as possible – then stand back and watch it soar!

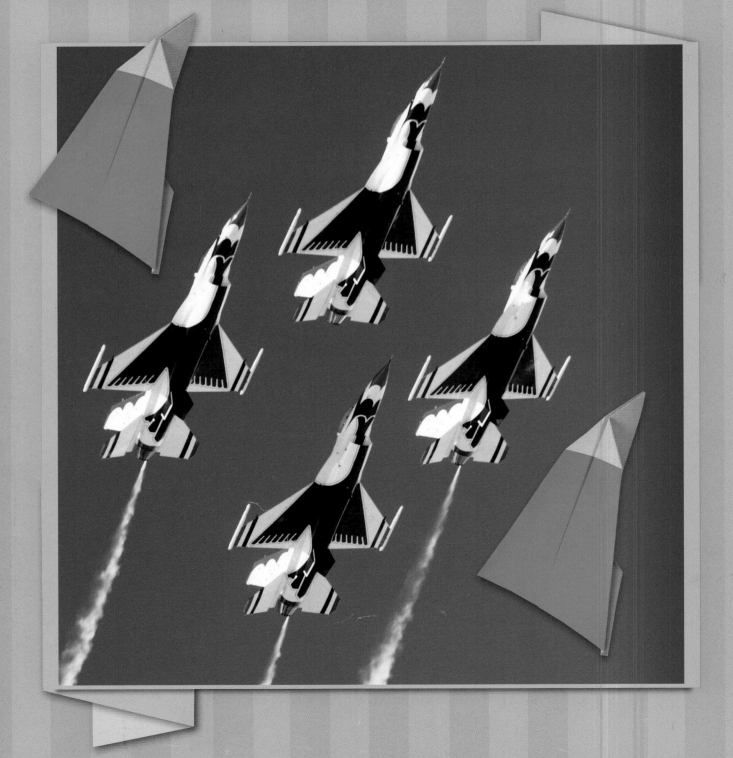

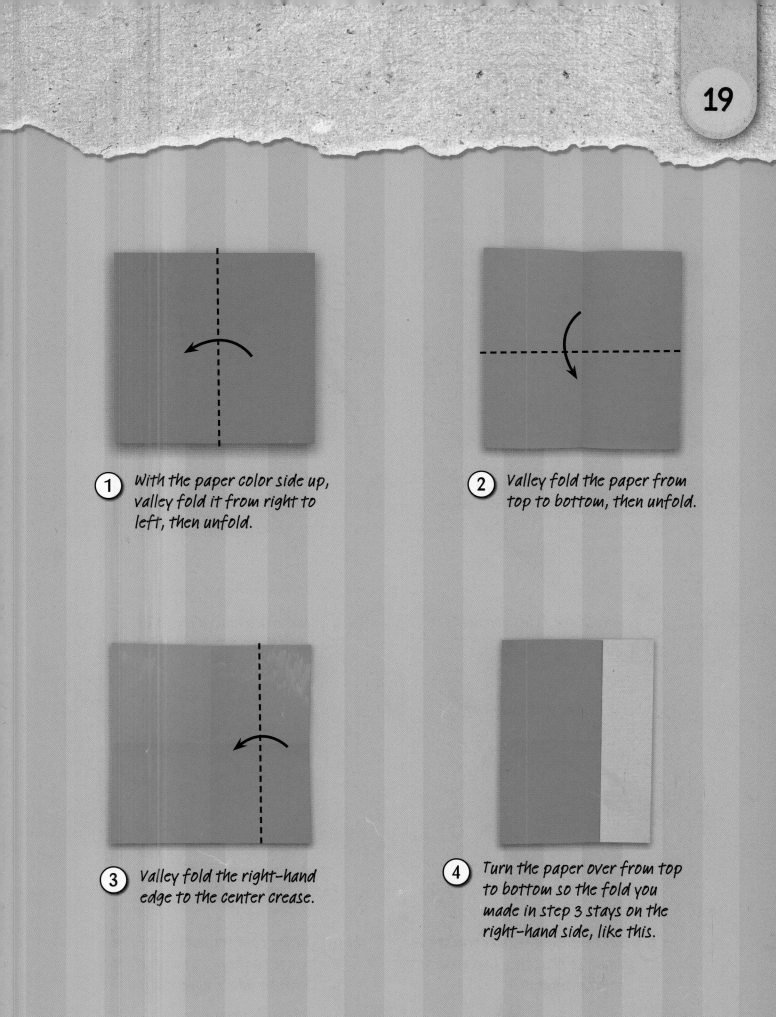

1. With the paper color side up, valley fold it from right to left, then unfold.

2. Valley fold the paper from top to bottom, then unfold.

3. Valley fold the right-hand edge to the center crease.

4. Turn the paper over from top to bottom so the fold you made in step 3 stays on the right-hand side, like this.

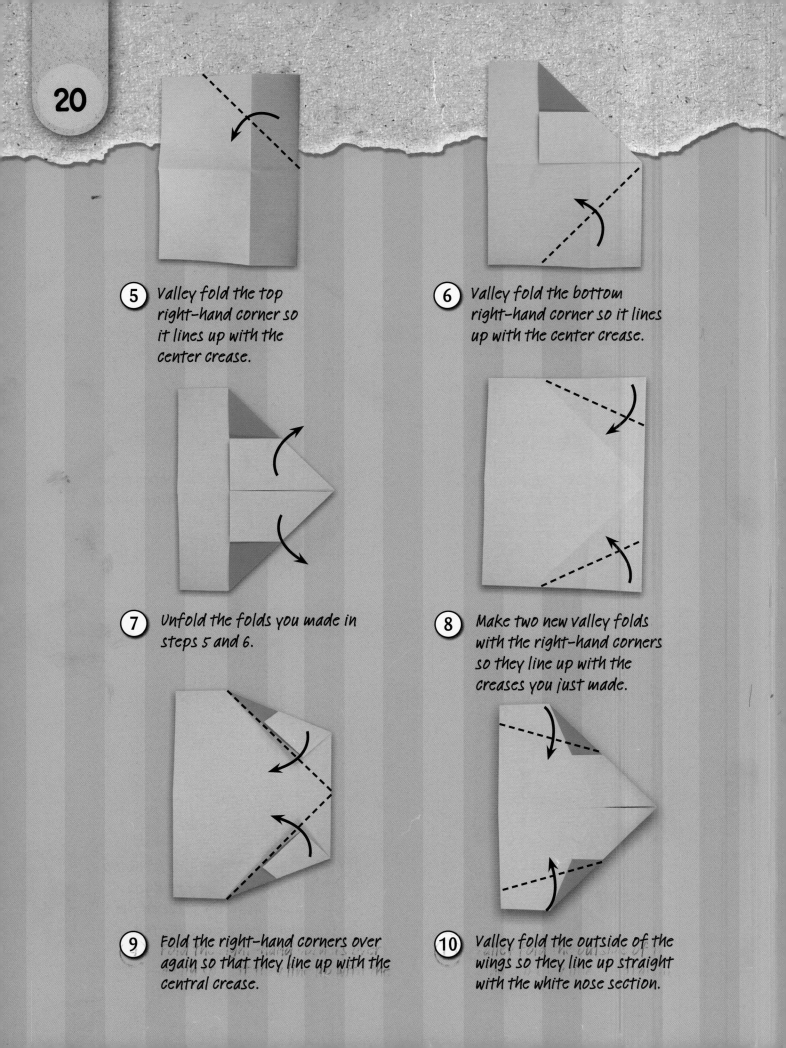

5 Valley fold the top right-hand corner so it lines up with the center crease.

6 Valley fold the bottom right-hand corner so it lines up with the center crease.

7 Unfold the folds you made in steps 5 and 6.

8 Make two new valley folds with the right-hand corners so they line up with the creases you just made.

9 Fold the right-hand corners over again so that they line up with the central crease.

10 Valley fold the outside of the wings so they line up straight with the white nose section.

Valley fold the rear of the wings so they line up with the outside edges.

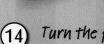 Mountain fold the paper in half along the central crease.

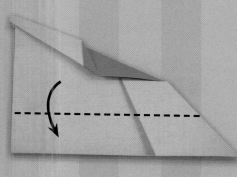 Valley fold the top wing down, as shown.

Turn the paper over.

 Repeat step 13 on the other side and your model is nearly complete.

 Unfold the wings, even them up, and your plane is ready to take to the skies.

Flying Valentine

Make it a Valentine's Day to remember by creating this cute flying heart card. Then send it over to that special someone – without them knowing, of course!

1 Position the paper like this, white side up. Valley fold the paper in half but don't crease it.

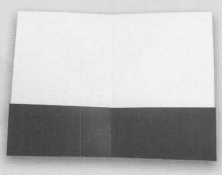

2 Just pinch the middle to show where the halfway point is. Then valley fold the bottom half of the paper to the middle point and crease.

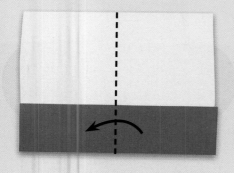

3 Fold the paper in half from right to left, but again don't crease.

4 Gently pinch the paper at the bottom to show where the middle point is. Turn the paper over from left to right.

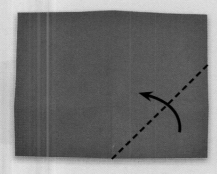

5 Fold the bottom right corner to the center, using the pinch mark as a guide.

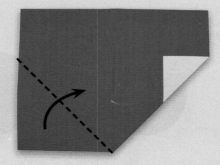

6 Fold the bottom left corner to the center, again using the pinch mark as a guide.

⑦ Rotate your paper so the pointed end is facing away from you, then turn it over from right to left.

⑧ Valley fold the top point so it's about 3/4 inch (2 cm) from the bottom edge.

Push

⑨ Your paper should look like this. Turn it over from left to right.

⑩ Use your finger to open up the flap in the top right corner to form a pocket.

Push

⑪ Flatten the pocket to form a triangular shape, like this.

⑫ Now, use your finger to open up the flap in the top left corner to form a pocket.

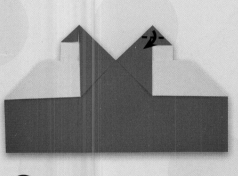

13 Flatten the pocket to form a triangular shape. Then make a small diagonal fold in the top right corner.

14 Make a small diagonal fold in the top left corner.

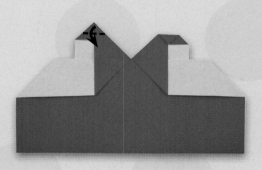

15 Fold over the top right point.

16 Fold over the top left point.

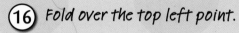

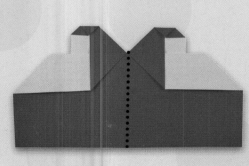

17 Your paper should now look like this. Mountain fold it down the middle.

18 Turn your paper over and open it up. Your Valentine heart is ready to fly to that special someone!

Helicopter

You may get dizzy watching this super spinning copter whirling around. The higher you drop it, the more it will spin!

1. Place the paper with the white side facing down and a straight edge facing towards you.

2. Valley fold the paper in half from right to left, then unfold.

3. Valley fold the paper in half from top to bottom, then unfold.

4. Turn the paper over. Then valley fold the paper in half diagonally from right to left.

5. Your paper should look like this.

Push ◄

Push ◄

(6) Unfold the paper and turn it so the diagonal fold made in step 4 is now horizontal.

(7) Start pushing the sides together so the paper starts folding up.

(8) The paper should fold itself into a square. With the open side facing you, valley fold the top layer of the paper in half.

(9) Your paper should look like this. Turn the paper over from left to right.

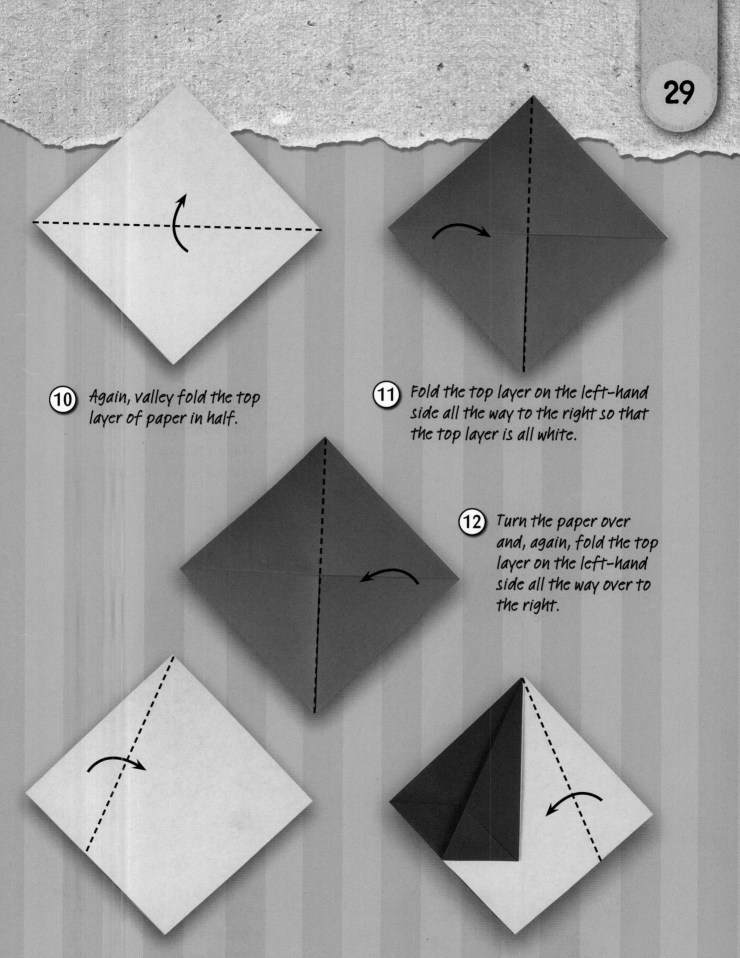

10 Again, valley fold the top layer of paper in half.

11 Fold the top layer on the left-hand side all the way to the right so that the top layer is all white.

12 Turn the paper over and, again, fold the top layer on the left-hand side all the way over to the right.

13 Diagonally fold the top left layer to the center line.

14 Diagonally fold the top right layer to the center line.

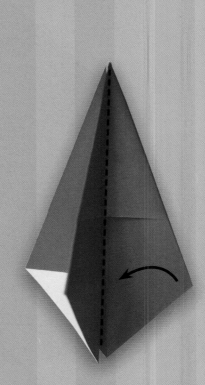

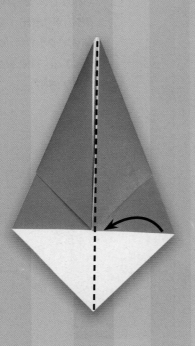

(15) Your paper should look like this. Turn it over.

(16) Fold the left-hand side into the center line, like this. Then fold the right-hand side into the center line.

(17) Fold the top right-hand layer over to the left so there's no more white showing.

(18) Turn the paper over. Again, fold the top right-hand layer over to the left so there's no more white showing.

19 There should now be a clear gap in the bottom half of the paper. Valley fold the right flap up to the top.

20 Mountain fold the left-hand flap up to the top.

21 Pull the flaps out so they're pointing in opposite directions, like this.

22 Hold the helicopter with the two flaps at the top, gently release it and watch it spin.

Glossary

amethyst Either a violet or purple color, or a precious stone of that color.

crease A line in a piece of paper made by folding.

Mexico A country which lies between the United States and Central America.

monarch A person who rules over a country or empire, such as a king or queen.

mountain fold An origami step where a piece of paper is folded so that the crease is pointing upwards, like a mountain.

silk Either a delicate, soft type of cloth made from thread produced by silkworms, or the thread itself.

step fold A mountain fold and valley fold next to each other.

streamlined Designed to move as quickly as possible through air or water.

valentine Either a card you send to someone on St. Valentine's Day, February 14th, or the person to whom you send a valentine card.

valley fold An origami step where a piece of paper is folded so that the crease is pointing downwards, like a valley.

Further Reading

Akass, Susan. *My First Origami Book*. Cico Kidz, 2011.
Ard, Catherine. *Amazing Origami: Paper Planes*. Gareth Stevens Publishing, 2015.
Robinson, Nick. *The Awesome Origami Pack*. Barron's Educational Series, Inc., 2014.

Index